You're Moving on to 6th Grade!

Ways to Ease Your Transition into Middle School

Cynthia Bohannon-Brown, Ed. M.

ISBN: 069290865X
ISBN-13: 978-0692908655 (PEP HOUSE PRESS, Atlanta, GA.)

Interior images are under license from Shutterstock.com.

DEDICATED TO:

Past, Present, and Future Rising 6th Grade Students

With SPECIAL places in my heart for the students who INSPIRED this book:

Lamisa
Miguel
Jimena
Cynthia
Katie
Axel
Andrea
Johan
Irvin
Jesus
Cristopher
Melissa
Ryan
Alondra
Oscar
Stephanie
Nicole
Yovany
Melanie
Janet
&
Brandon

TABLE OF CONTENTS

An Introduction

Dear Rising 6th Grader,

CONGRATULATIONS, YOU DID IT! You have changed from a 5th grade student who needed much help with school work into a future 6th grade student who has learned to use different resources to find your own answers. You should really be proud of yourself for becoming a more confident and independent learner. You are ready for middle school.

Naturally, a few concerns about moving to the next level of learning may be on your mind. Leaving a smaller school to attend a larger one may feel a little uncomfortable. Leaving teachers that you have known for many years may be a bit frightening. With a little time and a few words of guidance, you may find that your transition won't be as scary as you had first thought.

As you read this book, ***You're Moving on to 6th Grade! Ways to Ease Your Transition into Middle School***, it may help to calm your fears. You will find guiding thoughts to help with situations in your new school. Use this book as a resource until you feel more comfortable handling your middle school experiences.

Right now, you may think that you're on your own and may feel a bit unsure. However, you will NEVER be truly alone. You will keep in touch with some of your old friends and meet new ones. Your parents, teachers, and other adults will be there to help you. By gaining more knowledge and experience about this transition, your confidence will likely increase.

As you begin middle school, know that your elementary teachers will always be willing to listen to you and will help you to find answers as well. Keep in mind that you will continue to be in our most positive thoughts throughout and beyond your 6th grade year.

Wishing you the best school year... EVER!

Your Elementary Teacher

Cynthia Bohannon-Brown, Ed. M.

Guiding Thought 1:
Get to Know the Adults in Your School

Teachers are only some of the adults in your new middle school.

People may seem to be EVERYWHERE on your first day of middle school! It will seem that way because students from nearby elementary schools will be brought together to create a larger middle school. Things may get very confusing when there are so many students in one school building. However, your new middle school will likely have more school personnel or adults to help with the crowds of students as well. The faculty, staff, and administrators will be there to help you make a smooth transition from elementary to middle school.

On the first day, you will notice students trying to find their classes. You may see the office staff answering questions for parents while teachers stand in their classroom doorways. Your school's principal may walk throughout the building to make sure that the campus is safe and orderly. As a new student, you may have questions or need help. Knowing who to turn to for answers will be a very important part of becoming a responsible 6th grade student.

Even though you've spent many years in elementary school, you may not understand each adult's role in your building. As a middle school student, you will need to know the administrators, faculty, and staff as soon as possible. They will be responsible for answering your questions. By the time you receive your first progress report, about four weeks after school starts, you should be able to identify the jobs and the names of each adult in your middle school.

MIDDLE SCHOOL FACULTY AND STAFF

Middle School Principal (Administrator)
<ul><li>is responsible for the daily operation of the middle school</li><li>ensures the safety of everyone in the building</li><li>cares for the emotional and physical well-being of all students in the school</li></ul>

Your principal will be responsible for the smooth operation of the entire school. He or she will ensure that all teachers, staff, and students do their parts to make each school day a positive learning experience. This adult will represent your school in the community. Your principal should maintain a safe and respectful environment for everyone in your new middle school.

Assistant Principal (Administrator)
• serves as a co-leader and acts as a role model for faculty, staff and students • is responsible for the school environment in the principal's absence • cares for the emotional and physical well-being of all students in the school

Another middle school adult will be your assistant principal. He or she will work to support the principal and will complete assigned tasks. When your principal is away from school, the assistant principal will manage the faculty, staff, and students. Along with the principal, the assistant principal will be a part of your school's administration team.

Teachers (faculty)
*This category includes general education, as well as P.E., Art, Music/Band, Technology, ESOL (English to Speakers of Other Languages), Special Education and other teachers.
• guide students through approved course content or information • use homework, quizzes, and tests to guide students' learning • care for the emotional and physical well-being of all students in the class/school

In 6th grade, you will have five to six classes each day. Each classroom teacher will guide you through one subject area, such as science, social studies, English/language arts, and mathematics. You will have teachers responsible for band, sports teams, clubs, and other types of groups. Also, there will be teachers who will work with special programs, such as Special Education and English to Speakers of Other Languages (ESOL).

Media Specialist (Faculty)
• manages the use of most technology resources • trains faculty, staff, parents, and students on the proper use of printed materials and technology tools • cares for the emotional and physical well-being of all students in the class/school

Your media specialist will be another teacher in your middle school. He or she will teach you about resources found in the media center, including printed materials and technology (tech) tools. Those tech tools may be desktop and laptop computers as well as smaller tablets. Your media specialist will provide support materials to help teachers with instruction. Also, he or she will help you to locate research information for projects. Your media specialist will be a very helpful resource next school year.

Counselor (Staff)
• cares for the emotional and physical well-being of all students in the school • helps students with problems dealing with other people and their personal feelings • listens to any concerns about stressful situations at home or at school

Your middle school counselor will work with students who are experiencing stressful situations. With the changes next school year, you may need extra support. You may need to speak with your counselor:

- when you have a difficult time making friends,
- when you have issues at home or at school,
- when you are confused and need someone to listen to your thoughts and feelings,
- when you need someone to share in your excitement or concern about getting your progress reports or report cards, and
- when someone else needs help, but doesn't know how to ask for it.

After your school year starts, you may think of more ways that your counselor may help you. When you have a chance, introduce yourself to your 6th grade counselor. He or she will find time to speak with students during the school year.

Social Worker (Staff)
- identifies community resources based on the needs of students and their families - cares for the emotional and physical well-being of all students in the school

Your school social worker will be another adult who will help with difficult and stressful situations. He or she will work with the counselor.

When situations at home affect you at school, the social worker may become involved. If you are absent or tardy from school for too many days, he or she will visit your home to check on you. The social worker may contact community organizations, like a food pantry, to help families in need. The social worker will be available to help students in your community.

Front Office Staff
• is key to good communication between the school's administrators, teachers, students, parents, and the community • sends letters and notes to parents about school events • cares for the emotional and physical well-being of all students in the school

The front office will be the main communication center for your middle school. The principal's office will be located in or around that area. Your school's secretary and other staff will work in the front office. The secretary may be the first person to greet people when they enter the building. He or she will make sure that all visitors check into the office before going to other parts of the school. The secretary will be responsible for: enrolling and unenrolling students, requesting and transferring records, accepting all mail, and answering questions in person, by phone, or by email. The secretary will assist your principal with information that needs to be sent to parents. In the absence of the school nurse, the secretary may be the person to help students.

In schools with parents who speak languages other than English, an interpreter may work in the front office, too. The interpreter will speak with parents in their native language, and then repeat the conversation in English for other people. When someone answers in English, the interpreter will explain it to parents in their native language. This cycle will continue until everyone involved understands the information being shared. The interpreter will be able to write or translate letters from English into the parents' native language as well.

Many school districts provide free interpretation and translation services for parents. For parent-teacher conferences, the interpreter may be requested by parents or by teachers. Interpreters will ensure clear communication between the administrators, faculty, staff, students, and parents who speak languages other than English.

Nurse (Staff)
<ul><li>helps students and adults who are ill (sick) or injured (hurt)</li><li>informs students about ways to stay healthy</li><li>cares for the emotional and physical well-being of all students in the school</li></ul>

Your middle school nurse will collect and update information about the health of all students. The nurse may give you medicine prescribed by a doctor while at school. This adult will make sure that all types of medicine are stored safely in locked cabinets.

If you get hurt, the nurse will give you first-aid. Also, the nurse will decide if you are too sick to remain at school. He or she will be trained to help in emergency medical situations and will call for emergency assistance, if needed. Your school nurse will be important to the physical well-being of everyone in your middle school.

SRO Staff
(School **R**esource **O**fficers)

- works with administrators, staff, teachers, parents, and students to maintain a safe school environment
- talks with students about concerns about safe/unsafe behavior or situations
- cares for the emotional and physical well-being of all students in the school

School resource officers (SROs) will be law enforcement staff placed in your school to keep everyone safe. SROs must follow all laws and will usually wear special uniforms. These adults will have received special training to carry and to use weapons. SROs will make sure that all students follow your school's rules. They may teach you about ways to help prevent emergency situations. Along with the custodians, SROs will help to keep all exits secured. In case of an emergency situation, they will work with the administrators, faculty, staff, and the local police department to quickly get it under control. These adults will help to create a safe learning environment for you.

Custodians (Staff)
• ensure the safety of the school environment (all areas of the building and the school grounds) • keep all areas clean and in good working order • care for the emotional and physical well-being of all students in the school

At the beginning of each school day, the custodians will unlock the doors and turn off the security alarm. They will check to ensure that there are not any dangerous situations in the building or on the school grounds. The custodians will work to prevent accidents. If something needs to be repaired, they will be the adults for that job.

Custodians will ensure that your classrooms, restrooms, and hallways are clean and safe to use. They will check to see that all lights are in working condition and that the floors are free from trash and spills. Also, custodians may handle jobs like moving desks into classrooms for new students and carrying technology equipment into the media center. Sometimes, they will work beyond their times to go home. This may happen if they are needed to set up for school dances and other after school events.

During emergency situations, your custodians will work with the other adults in the building to make sure that everyone is safe. At the end of the day, custodians will check the building and the school grounds, set the alarm, and lock the doors before leaving to go home. Your new middle school will operate smoothly with the help of its custodians.

Cafeteria Staff
<ul><li>serves balanced meals (breakfast and lunch) in a timely manner</li><li>ensures that all children eat breakfast and lunch each day</li><li>cares for the emotional and physical well-being of all students in the school</li></ul>

The cafeteria staff's school days will begin well before teachers and students arrive. Cafeteria workers will be responsible for preparing all school meals eaten by you and your peers. They will store perishable food items, which need to be refrigerated or frozen, in their proper places. Cafeteria workers will make sure that food items are kept at the correct temperatures, so that you will not get sick. These adults will ensure that non-perishable items, which do not need to be refrigerated or frozen, are stored properly in cool, clean areas. Also, they will make sure that their work spaces are clean at all times.

Cafeteria workers will ensure that all students have a chance to eat breakfast and lunch. If you do not have money to pay for your meals, they will allow you to eat. However, the cafeteria manager will send a letter to your parents about any money that you owe. Cafeteria workers will make sure that your meals are served in a timely manner, so that you can get to your next class on time.

Bookkeeper (Staff)
• maintains information about money or funds for the school • is responsible for collecting all funds for field trips • cares for the emotional and physical well-being of all students in the school

Your school's bookkeeper will not usually work directly with students. However, he or she may be assigned to help the front office staff. The bookkeeper will handle money from school activities. When a school fundraiser takes place, this adult will collect money from your teachers, deposit the funds into the bank, and keep track of the total amount.

The bookkeeper will make sure that faculty and staff are paid for the number of days worked. He or she will ensure that all bills are paid when items are purchased by the school. The bookkeeper will make sure that all of the school's funds are handled correctly.

Bus Drivers (Staff)
• safely drive school buses • maintain a safe school bus environment • care for the emotional and physical well-being of all students on the bus

The main job of your school bus driver will be to get you and other students safely to school, to and from field trips, and back home. He or she will make sure that the school bus is safe to drive. The driver will check the bus to make sure that all parts are working properly. If something needs to be fixed, then the driver will report it to the transportation office and get it fixed as soon as possible. If an emergency repair is needed, then he or she will request another bus. Also, the bus driver will practice getting you safely off the bus during emergency drills.

Your bus driver will ensure your safety while traveling down crowded roadways each day. He or she will be trained to handle the school bus in many different weather conditions. Your bus driver will monitor the behavior of all students using a large mirror located above the windshield of the bus.

As a school bus rider, you will be able to help your driver with bus safety. You will need to act in a safe manner by obeying all rules, staying seated, and talking quietly. Remember that your safe actions will allow your bus driver to concentrate on driving the school bus each day.

More Thoughts about School Personnel

- *Middle school adults are people, too.*

   Get to know school personnel by their names. Addressing them as Mr., Mrs., Ms., Dr., or Coach, followed by their last names, will show respect for the jobs that they perform. The administrators, faculty and staff will work with many middle school students. Keep in mind that there will be times when adults may forget your name or call you the name of another student. You may need to repeat your name several times before it will be remembered. In time, the adults will get to know you and recognize other qualities that make you a unique student.

Be mindful that middle school adults will have emotions and issues just like you. There may be a time when an adult will show signs of stress. He or she may speak in a louder tone, seem to have less patience, or act in a grumpy manner. In these instances, you will need to give that adult time to deal with an issue that may not involve you. You will need to show respectful behavior. Calmly walk away and find another time to talk to that person. You may choose to find another adult to help you. For questions about classwork, you may ask other responsible students. The way in which you handle difficult situations, especially with adults, will show that you respect others and yourself.

- *Middle school adults are NOT your friends.*

You may find adults that you think are great people. They may listen to you and even laugh at funny situations with you. You will find that some adults will give you helpful advice and may be friendly. However, middle school adults will not be your friends. Your friends will be the other students in your school. When you speak with your friends, your conversations may be about school, your personal likes and dislikes, and things related to being a teenager. On the other hand, the adults in your school will be advisors who will guide you through situations. When talking to adults, your conversations may focus more on classwork or school activities, on concerns or issues, and on ways that you can become a better student. The relationships that you will create with adults will be different from those that you will create with other students next year.

If you feel unsure or uncomfortable about a situation with someone, simply share it with your parents and your counselor. By asking the advice of other trusted adults, you may get a clearer understanding about the correctness of any relationship.

- ***Middle school adults are excellent resources.***

The issues that you will face in middle school will not be new ones. However, they will be new to you. The faculty and staff will have many more years of experience. They will have suggestions to help you with most issues. Once you find someone that you trust, listen to their advice.

The most important jobs for middle school administrators, faculty, and staff will be to ensure the academic, emotional, and physical well-being of all students. Academic well-being includes understanding your classwork. Emotional well-being includes understanding your feelings and handling situations in positive ways. Physical well-being includes making sure that you are healthy and safe at home and at school. Helping you with academic, emotional, and physical concerns will be the main tasks of all school personnel. Allow them to do their jobs during your first year of middle school.

Guiding Thought 2:

Learn Your School Building and its Environment

A school map shows the location of hallways and classrooms.

Getting lost may be one of the worst feelings in the world. One minute you may be walking and shopping in a mall with family or friends. Then, you turn away for a few seconds only to look back and find that no one looks familiar. You're surrounded by strangers! Your heart begins to beat faster. You start taking shorter breaths. As you try to make sense of what just happened, your whole body tenses up. Fearful thoughts begin to take over your mind…UNTIL… you see a familiar face walking towards you. Instantly, your body relaxes. You inhale deeply and exhale with a loud sigh. An ear-to-ear smile takes over your face, as you think to yourself...*WHEW, what a relief!*

Leaving your elementary school for a new and unknown middle school may make you feel stressed just like the thought of being lost. However, going to middle school will not be a situation that happens all of a sudden. You have been preparing for this change for the past few months. You may have discussed it with your 5th grade teacher or even visited your local middle school on a field trip. Yet, you may still be a little bit concerned about entering a new building and not knowing the location of important places. While not being familiar with a new place may cause you to feel uncertain, keep in mind that it is just a building. It will have walls, windows, doors, and classrooms just like your elementary school. The main difference may be that your new school may be larger. However, you will get to know that building over time. Just be patient.

The middle school staff will expect you to be nervous about starting your 6th grade year. That is the purpose of a planned event called an orientation. This special program may take place during the summer or at the beginning of the new school year. During orientation, you will get a chance to visit the school and meet new classmates as well as some of the faculty and staff. You will participate in activities designed to teach you about the expectations for 6th grade students. Look for information about the orientation in the mail or visit your middle school's website.

Sometimes information about orientation will be mailed to the address that was given to your elementary school. Make sure that your address has been updated with your elementary school's front office staff before you leave for summer break. If you are unsure, you or your parents may call to double-check. If your address has not been corrected, you may not get information sent about middle school events during the summer. Also, you may end up going to the wrong middle school. Be mindful that the selection of your new middle school will be based on your current home address.

If you wish to get familiar with your new building before orientation, simply stop by the middle school to pick up a map. Having one may help ease your worries. A map of the school will show you hallways, classrooms, and other important areas. You should plan to visit the school as close to the end or the beginning of the school year as possible. Keep in mind that the summer months will be times when most students and teachers will not be in the building. During that break, custodians will move around furniture and deep clean all areas of the building, including carpets, floors, and even the walls. Only a few personnel will work during the summer, so you may want to call before visiting.

When you visit the school, if a map is not available, you and your parents may ask if you can take a walk around the building. This will give you time to draw your own map. You may wish to include important areas, such as the main entrance, main office, 6th grade classrooms, the cafeteria, and the bus lanes. You may wish to add the media center, gym, and any outdoor areas that are used during the school day. If you have time, mark all emergency exits or doors that lead to the outside. Later, you may want to identify any interior or enclosed courtyard areas as well. The doors that lead to those areas will not be considered emergency exits because they are usually completely surrounded by walls or a fence. Those areas may cause you to be trapped during an emergency, such as a fire. True emergency exits will allow you to leave the school building and move safely to another location to wait for help to arrive. Make sure that your map has all of the important areas of the school building. It is important that your map will have the location of places visited by 6th grade students. If you have older friends or family members who attend the same middle school, ask them to help add details to it. A map will be an important tool for you next school year.

Keep in mind that your map does not have to be perfect and that you will not be graded on it. You may need it only for the first few weeks of school. Before long, you will be able to move around the building with ease.

Guiding Thought 3:
Prepare for Learning

Being organized will help you prepare for your classes.

After you have attended an orientation, met some of the faculty and staff, and studied your map of the school, you will need to attend your classes. A schedule of classes will be given to you. It will show the course names, their starting and ending times, their locations, and the names of your teachers. As soon as you get your schedule, write all of that information in a notebook. Making a copy of it will help if you misplace or lose it.

On the first day of school, imagine that you made it to all of your classes on time. For the next couple of days, you were the first student to arrive at three of your classes. However, on the fourth day, you made it to your Math class with only a few seconds to spare because you stopped to talk to a friend in the hallway. As your teacher closes the door, you realize that you forgot to stop by your locker to get your Math book, notes, and homework! How will you explain this issue to your teacher and what grade will you earn? A similar situation may happen when you get to middle school. To give you a better understanding about some possible middle school issues, an informal survey was given to 76 sixth grade students. They shared their thoughts about a few questions, such as **What's the hardest part of changing classes each day?** Here are their top three responses.

Twenty-seven Responses: Being on Time for Class

The students shared that the hardest part of changing classes was getting to class on time. Once in middle school, you will have a set amount of time between classes. You may feel a little stressed because it may take five minutes to simply walk from one class to another one. If other things happen along the way, then you may be late for class. Let's look at some things that may cause you to lose that time and ways that you may be able to make it to class on time.

What if a teacher lets you out of class late? Leaving late means that you will have less than five minutes to make it to class. When it comes to instruction, each content area will have much information that you will need to learn. Therefore, it will be possible for a teacher to lose track of time during instruction. Work with your classmates and teacher to find a solution. Keeping up with the time may become the job of a student. That student will let the teacher know when a few minutes remain. Together, all of you may think of other creative ways to signal that instruction will soon be over. Remember to present all suggestions with respect. This will help you to create positive student-teacher relationships.

Another factor that may keep you from getting to class on time may be the distance between your classes. Sometimes your classes will be closer to each other and arriving on time will not be an issue. However, what will happen when one class is farther away? You will stand a really good chance of being late if you do not have a plan in mind. You will need to share your concern with your teachers. A possible solution may be for you to create a daily hall pass for the teacher to sign. It will need to include your name, the date and time as well as the location of your next class. Your pass will allow you to leave class a couple of minutes early. Those extra minutes may mean the difference between arriving on time and arriving late. Keep in mind that the hallways will be monitored by adults, such as SROs. They will make sure that you have permission to be out of class by checking your hall pass. Keep in mind that your pass should only be used to get you from one class to another one. Stopping at another location, such as the restroom or your locker, will not be a good choice. You will need to go directly to your next class to show that you are able to be trusted. Once in your next class, you may get your teacher's permission to go somewhere else.

With only about five minutes between classes, you may not have time to visit your locker, stop by the restroom, or talk to friends. In the case of your locker needs, you may plan to take the materials for your first two to three classes with you at the beginning of your day. During your scheduled breaks or before lunch, you may be able to exchange your books and materials from the morning with those that you will need for your afternoon classes. Use your class schedule to decide when you will visit your locker.

Finding time to use the restroom may cause you to be late for class as well. However, if it is an emergency, then you will need to go and simply explain it to your teacher later. Be mindful that most middle school restrooms will not be monitored by an adult. Pay careful attention when using those areas. You may ask a friend to go with you and take turns watching each other's backpack. If it is not an emergency situation, you may ask the teacher for a pass after you arrive in class on time. By the time your class starts, most students should be out of the restrooms.

If you enter a crowded restroom, you may choose to wait outside for some of the students to leave. Also, you may come back when it is less crowded or simply find another restroom to use. Usually, adults will monitor the hallways. If an emergency happens in the restroom and you cannot leave, shout the letters "S.R.O.!" or the word

"Teacher!" over and over again until someone comes to help you. Be mindful of unsafe situations in school. Have a plan to keep yourself safe at all times. Your well-being will be important to all adults in your middle school.

Another action that may make you late for class is stopping to talk with your friends in the hallway. Instead of the hallway, you may find time to talk to them on the bus, during breakfast and lunch, or at home. Talking to your friends in the hallway will not be a good reason to be late for class. Your friends should understand the importance of getting to class on time, too. Being focused on your attendance will be a great way to begin your 6th grade year.

After all of your planning, if tardiness becomes an issue, talk with your teachers and your counselor. When visiting your counselor's office, write down your concern ahead of time. You can leave the note if he or she is not available to speak with you. Include the date and the time that you left it. Record that information in the back of your class notebook.

The office staff or the school secretary will be able to get the note to the counselor. Keep in mind that he or she will be responsible for many other students, too. When time is available, the counselor will contact you about your note. If you don't get an answer in a couple of days, you may need to find another time to check directly with him or her. Remember to keep your parents aware of any tardiness and make sure that they write a note to explain each day that you are absent.

That documentation will let the office staff know that you were out of school for a reason and not absent without permission. Keeping track of attendance and all communications with adults will show your parents and teachers that you are becoming a more responsible student.

In all of the examples given to prevent being late for class, communication has been a part of every solution. Keep all of your teachers aware of things that help or prevent you from getting to class as expected. Your voice will be your most powerful tool. After all, it will be your responsibility to let others know what you need in 6th grade.

Eighteen Responses: Crowds in the Hallway

According to the survey, a large number of students in the hallway was the second hardest thing about changing classes. Some middle schools may seem like small cities because they contain more than a thousand students. Unlike in your elementary school, many middle school students may not be expected to walk in single file lines, one behind the other, in the hallways. Their lines will seldom seem straight, except in the cafeteria serving lines. Because many students will use the hallways at the same time, it may become a bit congested and difficult to travel. However, by learning the building, you may be able to quickly plan the best and safest routes between classes. Remember to use the map that you picked up from school or the one that you created.

(See: Guiding Thought 2, pages 28-29.)

Once you observe the hallways, you will notice the directions in which the students will travel. If most students are walking down the middle of the hallway, you can walk closer to the walls to pass by them. If most of them stand closer to the walls or lockers, then you may carefully make your way down the center of the hallway. If neither of those choices work, then you may need to take another way around the crowd, if possible. Sometimes, you may need to simply move aside and wait until you see a safe way through the crowd. Observe the hallway traffic and be prepared to make the safest choice for each new situation.

During the first week of school, check with your classmates to see if they share any other classes with you. If so, you may want to become hallway buddies and work together to get through the crowds. By the end of your first month of school, expect to have your route worked out.

Be aware that crowds in the hallway may create other problems. Getting into an incident may make you late for class. In a rush, you may accidentally hit another student with your backpack. That student may feel angry about being hit. Those feelings may turn into an argument or worse, a fight! To reduce those chances, you will need to quickly apologize and check to make sure the person is not hurt. By apologizing as soon as it happens, you will show that hitting the student was not done on purpose. Sometimes, there will be no way to prevent bumping into others. Simply do your best to avoid it. Remember to use respectful words, like "Excuse me", if it happens and take care getting through the crowded hallways.

Most of the time, you will be able to handle hallway situations on your own. If you see an argument or a fight in a hallway, move away from those involved as quickly and as safely as possible. Then, go to class. Stopping to watch a situation will not be a good excuse for being late. Sometimes students who are watching may end up involved in it. Also, fewer students in the hallways may help adults to quickly end an incident. School resource officers (SROs) may be located throughout your school building and will likely be the first adults available to stop an argument or a fight.

Remember that many arguments and fights can be prevented. Calmly discussing issues with other students may be one way to avoid an argument. Do your best to find peaceful solutions to any problem. If you cannot handle a situation, ask for help. Teachers and your counselor will be there to assist with settling issues between students. If you learn about an unsafe situation, share it privately with a teacher and a school resource officer (SRO). Keep in mind that as a school citizen, you will be responsible for helping to keep yourself and others safe.

Nine Responses: Organization

The third hardest thing about changing classes, for some 6th grade students, was organization of materials.

In 5th grade, you may have stayed in one classroom and had only one main teacher. Your materials were stored in desks that were assigned to you for the whole school year. Keeping up with your things will be different in middle school. In 6th grade, you may not return to a homeroom class at the end of the day. Therefore, you will be responsible for keeping up with all of your items.

Some schools will provide lockers for you, while others may not have lockers at all. When using a locker, you will need to have a plan. The first thing that you will need is a lock to secure your things inside of your locker. There are two kinds of locks available: locks with keys and locks with combinations. If you buy a lock with a key, you will need to keep the key from getting lost, stolen, or misplaced. This can be done by zipping it inside a special section of your backpack. You will need it each time you want to enter your locker. On the other hand, with a combination lock, you will have to remember a series of numbers in order to open your locker. Sometimes, combination locks may not open on the first try. Other times, numbers may be forgotten, so write them down in your notebook. You may ask your middle school friends for suggestions about what type of lock to use. Remember that the final decision will be up to you.

When you are assigned a locker, only store your items inside. Your friends should have their own lockers. Never allow anyone to have the key or the combination to it. Never hold things for others in your locker. You will be responsible for anything found inside of it, whether the items belongs to you or not.

When using a locker, you will need to make sure that you can quickly get the right tools for each class. One suggestion may be to use a different color for each class. You can get colored labels from stores that sell school supplies. Also, you could get creative and make your own labels. Whatever you decide, you will need to make sure that the labels stick tightly to your materials.

If Math were your first class, you may choose to place a green tape or label on all of the things that will go with you to that class. The labels should be large enough for you to see it easily on each item. Select a different color for each of your other classes and color code all of those materials, too. Colored labels may make storing your things easier. You will simply place your materials inside your locker by color. When it is time to go to your Math class, you will place all of the green-labeled folders, notebooks, and textbook inside your backpack. Your new system will work the same way for your other classes.

For those students who will not have lockers, you will carry all textbooks and supplies with you each day. One good point about not having a locker may be that you can go straight from one class to another one. However, a backpack is much smaller than a locker, so you have less space to hold your things. Also, your backpack may get heavy. Buy one with comfortable shoulder straps.

When preparing your backpack, you will need to keep it organized for three reasons: 1) to easily get your things out of it, 2) to quickly and neatly put things back inside and 3) to make it easy to carry. If the items in your backpack are organized by color, it may be easier for you to manage. Simply use the same color coding system given for locker users and make it work for your backpack. You may wish to have a pouch or plastic bag for smaller things like pencils and erasers. The bag will prevent things from falling to the bottom of your backpack. Also, you may wish to have thin, single-subject spiral notebooks for each class. This will save time and space if you place the notebooks inside of your textbooks. Also, thinner notebooks will weigh less than thicker, bulkier ones.

To stay organized, you will need to put your materials back in your backpack as soon as you finish using them. Keep in mind that the end of each class period may include time to review the lesson, assign homework, and pack up your things. At that time, things may seem a little rushed. Organization of your tools will save you time and will allow you to quickly leave each class when given permission.

You may wish to have a system for staying organized at home, too. After you finish your nightly homework, plan to spend some time placing all of your school materials neatly in your backpack. To save time in the mornings, get your parents to check your homework, write notes, and sign all paperwork before going to bed. You will be able to add those things to your organized backpack, then place the backpack by the front doorway. If your parents are not able to check the information before you go to bed, simply place those items in a special place near your backpack. Your parents can complete the tasks and replace those items near your backpack. By having a special backpack area, it may make it easier to leave home each morning. By setting up a system for your materials at home and at school, you can stay organized throughout your entire 6th grade year.

The concerns from the student survey shared the thoughts of one group of 6th grade students. Every middle school environment will be different. In spite of that fact, the previous suggestions may help you to prepare for learning next year. Continue to look for other ways to get to class on time, to avoid the hallway crowds, and to keep your class materials organized once your 6th grade year begins.

Guiding Thought 4:
Understand Changes

Caterpillars undergo dramatic changes to become adult butterflies.

Before you left elementary school, you celebrated your promotion to middle school with your teachers, classmates, and parents. You may have received awards or had ice cream and cake to mark your accomplishments. Leaving 5th grade represented one of the biggest changes in your life. With that transition, you are moving closer to becoming an adult. Adulthood begins when you are 18 years old. However, you are not there yet! Your next level in middle school will prepare you for high school, and then high school will prepare you for adulthood.

Your first year in middle school will include many changes. Some of them will happen without any warning, while you will know when other changes are taking place. As you become more aware of certain changes, simply do your best to handle them as positively as possible.

~ *Changes in Your Dependency Level*~

In elementary school, you may have depended on your parents to do many things for you. In middle school, you will be expected to accept more responsibility. Showing that you can do more things for yourself will become a very important part of your middle school life. Your new responsibilities may include setting your own alarm clock, so that you can get to school on time. Also, your parents may not be able to leave work to handle every issue that will arise at school. Therefore, you will need to speak up, share your concerns, and fully explain the type of support that you will need to become a better student. You may need to talk with your teachers to get more practice with classwork. Communicating with a teacher may include writing a note asking for help, and then continuing to check for an answer. By accepting more responsibility, you will show that you are becoming an even more independent middle school student.

Next school year, you will need to follow your school's rules and expectations with fewer directions from adults. A student handbook should be given to you. The handbook may include rules about your clothing, bullying, and truancy or being out of school without permission. Also, the handbook will explain the consequences for breaking school rules. It will be your responsibility to read, understand, and follow the rules.

You and your parents may be required to sign and return a form stating that you have read and understand everything in the handbook. Even if you choose not to read it, you will still be responsible for following the school rules and meeting the expectations. Plan to review the handbook with your parents. This may help them to fully understand your new role as a middle school student. Also, it may give your parents ideas about additional ways to support you. They may wish to get the phone numbers of other parents, so that they can create a support group. Connecting with others may help your parents stay informed about school activities.

You may wish to carry your student handbook in your backpack, so that you can review it when situations happen. If you have questions about your handbook, simply write them down. You may get answers during your orientation or later from your teachers and counselor. Also, you should review your middle school's website at the beginning of each week for more current information. Remember, it will be your responsibility to understand the rules and to meet the expectations of your new middle school.

~Changes in Your Style of Dress ~

Your parents may encourage you to choose which clothes to wear at home. However, in middle school, you may not have much choice about what you wear to class. Uniforms may be a part of your new school's expectations. Outfits may include a couple of colors and styles of shirts, pants, skirts, and dresses. Girls may be expected to wear uniform pieces that are not too short or too tight. Boys may be expected to use a belt to hold up their pants with their shirts tucked inside of them. Read your student handbook. As a 6th grade student, you will be expected to follow all rules about your new school's dress code.

If you must wear uniforms, you will have the freedom to find different ways to add to your uniform. You may wish to add interesting socks to your wardrobe or add a colorful tie, scarf, or belt. You may decide to wear really unique shoes. The ways in which you mix and match the pieces of your uniform will be totally up to you. School uniforms may make it easier to get dressed in the mornings because you will know exactly what to wear. You may even learn to enjoy adding to your outfits while meeting the expectations of your new middle school's dress code.

~Changes in Your School Work~

Your middle school will provide different ways for you to learn new skills away from your regular classes. You may get the chance to play an instrument in band class or sing in the chorus. The opportunity to learn French, Spanish, or another language may be a part of your additional classes. You may have the choice to participate in different sports such as soccer, basketball, and track. Clubs and other groups may be an option for you as well. Additional classes will provide time for you to learn many new skills. Usually, they are more relaxed than your regular academic classes. Your middle school will give you time to experience many new activities.

While those additional classes will be an important part of your school day, your regular classwork should be your main focus. Core classes such as English/language arts, math, science, and social studies will be important because they will prepare you for your 7th and 8th grade years in middle school.

Having more classes will mean that you will have more work, too. You will need to keep up with your daily classwork and homework. Be prepared to write notes while your teacher shares information. Ask questions during class time to make sure that you really understand the information. Some students may have the same questions, but are too shy to ask the teacher. If you are too shy to speak in class, write your teacher a note and give it to him or her before the end of class. This will give the teacher time to answer your question before you leave. For homework, be sure to write down your assignments completely and correctly. Check with other students to make sure that you have everything that you need before you leave each class. Homework is usually given to help you practice new skills. If you get behind in any of your work, it may become too difficult for you to keep learning new information. Before that happens to you, speak with your teachers and other classmates to find ways to handle the added workload. It will be impossible for you to get help if you do not ask for it. Allow your teachers and other classmates to help you become a well-informed 6th grade student.

~*Changes in Thoughts about Old Friends*~

Many of your elementary school friends may attend your new middle school. However, only some of them may take classes with you. This means that you may not get a chance to speak with your friends very much at school. Since you will have classes with other students, you and your old friends will probably make new friends, too. Simply because new friendships are being made does not mean that you and your old friends will not still be friends. Continue to speak to them and find time to keep in touch. You may wish to eat with them at lunch or you may decide to sit together on the school bus. You may wish to call them at home or make time to do homework together after school. There are many different ways to keep old friends while making new ones.

In middle school, you may realize that your new interests do not include some of your elementary school classmates. In some cases, neither you nor an old friend may wish to talk much to each other next year. However, plan to remain friendly towards him or her. In time, new friendships will develop and the old ones may not matter as much to you anymore.

If you are unable to reconnect with a friend and it becomes a problem for you or your friend, talk to a trusted teacher or to your school counselor. Talking to an adult may make it easier for you to understand your feelings about this change and may help you to move past it. Old friendships will need to be handled with care and respect, as you transition into middle school.

~*Changes in Your Thoughts about Making New Friends*~

Making new friends can be exciting. As you meet new people, you may want to be liked by them. However, certain classmates may realize this need in you and seek to take advantage of your feelings. They may strongly encourage you to do things that cause you to feel uncomfortable. Some peers may encourage you to break school rules. That kind of behavior is called negative peer pressure.

Negative peer pressure may lead you to do inappropriate things just to make or to keep friends. You may feel forced to follow your peers rather than listen to trusted adults or your parents. At some point, negative peer pressure may even turn into bullying. Bullying may happen if you are forced to do things that you don't want to do because you are afraid of someone. It may happen if someone treats you badly on a regular basis. This may cause you to feel depressed or sad. It will be important to stop such negative behavior as soon as possible. Ignoring this issue may only make it worse for you. If someone will bully you then he or she will probably do it to other students, too. Keep in mind that bullies will continue their behavior until someone cares enough to stop them. You may want to learn more about ways to stop bullying through an Internet resource, such as *Stopbullying.gov*.

As a student, you have the right to go to school without the stress caused by negative peer pressure and bullying. To get help, you will need to write down information and dates about each and every incident, so that you will be able to share it with adults. To stop this kind of behavior, you will need to speak to your parents, teachers, AND your school counselor. If you share your concern and nothing is done about the negative behavior, then you will have the right to speak with your principal or assistant principal about the situation. Your administrators are the main people who are responsible for your well-being during the school day. The administrators, faculty, and staff should make sure that you are safe at all times.

When choosing your friends, find classmates who practice positive peer interactions. Positive peer interactions happen when your friends strongly encourage you to do things that are helpful to you. It may include getting you to focus more on completing your assignments rather than choosing to play with others in class. It may include reminding you to go to class rather than standing in the hallway talking to other students. Keep in mind that true friends will suggest things that are helpful to you. They will set an example by following the rules. Friends will understand that you will make mistakes, but that you are still a special person.

Having true friends will include having a circle of caring and respectful peers who support you as you grow. Keep in mind that your friends can only give you suggestions about ways that you should act. Ultimately, your behavior will be your responsibility during your 6th grade year.

~ *Changes in Your Body and Mind* ~

Your middle school years represent the half-way point between childhood and adulthood. It will be like the pupa stage of a butterfly's life cycle when a caterpillar seals itself inside of a chrysalis. During that time, the caterpillar's body grows and changes. Then, it emerges as an adult butterfly. Your adolescent years will be your chrysalis stage. Many changes will take place in your body, your mind, and your life during your teenage years. These changes are a part of growing up. Certain changes may make you think, feel, act, or look differently. They may happen because of situations that you experience, new information that you learn, and the natural growth of your own body.

At some point, your body will begin to change and develop in new ways. Those changes are called puberty. Because your body is not the same as your friends' bodies, your physical changes will happen at a different rate. It may take place slower or quicker for you than for others. For some students, it may have happened as early as nine years old, while others may not see changes until their teenage years. Puberty will happen differently for boys than for girls. You may notice it when a boy's voice becomes deeper like a man's voice. Also, hair may begin to grow on his face and on other parts of his body. Puberty may be the time when a girl's body begins to develop in areas that make her look more like an adult woman. Hair may grow on other parts of her body as well. There are many different types of changes that may happen to your body.

Adolescence will be the time "from puberty to adulthood".[1] It will represent a time when you need to take extra special care of your body. The food that you will choose to eat and anything that you put into your body will affect its development. It will be like the time before a caterpillar entered the chrysalis stage. If the caterpillar had not eaten enough of the right food, it may not have had the energy that it needed to become a healthy adult butterfly. The same is true with your body. Healthy food will be important. Also, it will be important to keep dangerous things out of your body. Things like drugs or too much medicine will be harmful to you. You will need to care for and to respect your body, so that you can grow into a stronger, healthier person.

Your mind is a part of your body, too. It's the thinking part of your brain that includes your feelings. Even though your body's changes may make you look older, your emotions and thoughts may need time to grow and catch up with your body. In other words, you

1. "Stages of Adolescence." Healthy Children.org. https://www.healthychildren.org (June 30, 2017).

may think that you are grown in middle school, but it will take more years for your body and mind to completely develop into its adult state.

During your teenage years, you may begin to feel differently about other people as well. In elementary school, some girls may have only had friends who were girls. Some boys may have only had friends who were boys. When you get to middle school that may change. As your body changes, you may begin to feel differently about the opposite gender. Your gender identifies you as a girl (female) or a boy (male). In middle school, a boy may find that he likes being with one special girl and a girl may find that she enjoys talking to one special boy. Having friends who are of the opposite gender is a part of growing up, too. You and your friends may even discuss dating. However, keep in mind that teen dating is about becoming better friends and doing fun activities together, like skating or bowling. The more serious adult or grown-up dating is different. Adult dating will be something that you may decide to explore well after you leave middle school. In the meantime, you will become good friends with other students from both genders.

Thoughts about dating and changes in your body may seem confusing in middle school. Being in stressful situations may negatively affect your thoughts and emotions. It will be important for you to share your concerns with trusted adults. They may be able to share their own stories about ways that they made it through their own teenage years. Sharing your thoughts and listening to advice may cause you to feel less worried.

Less mental stress means that your body will feel less stressed, too.

Keep in mind that most of your older family members have already experienced adolescence. This means that you have others who are able to help you through this stage of life. Begin with your parents. Listen carefully to their advice even if other students choose not to listen to their parents. They will have a strong reason to help you. They have cared for you since birth and have seen you through other changes in your life. They will be supportive of you through these changes, too.

You may choose to speak to another trusted adult, such as a teacher, your school counselor, or another trusted faculty or staff member. Also, your family doctor will be a great resource to help with your physical changes. He or she has examined your body before and will have seen it develop over time. Your family doctor will be able to help explain the changes in your body.

If you find that you are nervous about asking for information about things like puberty, you may choose to use Internet resources. One resource for teens is an online magazine called *Choices* (http://www.choices.scholastic.com/). This resource discusses many topics, like personal health, relationships, and articles about real teens. *Choices* is published by Scholastic Incorporated (Inc.), which has written information for teachers and students for almost 100 years. Scholastic, Inc. is a reliable source for educational information online and in print.

Keep in mind that the information on all websites

may not be written by experts. Some of the advice and information may be incomplete or incorrect altogether. By sharing your resources with a trusted adult, you can double check the information for correctness.

~Changes in Your Knowledge about Technology Safety~

In elementary school, you were taught to safely use the World Wide Web (WWW) and the Internet for school work. As your use of technology grows, you may decide to connect with other people using social media, like Facebook or Twitter. It is important to be as careful with meeting people online as you are when you are walking down your neighborhood streets. Everything that people will share may not be the truth. People may pretend to be many things. Some people may pretend to be teenagers when they are actually adults. This lie or untruth may be shared to win your trust, so that they can get information about you and your family. Be careful not to give out any personal information. That information includes: your full name, your nickname, your address, the name of your school, your age, your phone number, the names of your family members, any social security numbers, and pictures. That information may be used to find you at your home or at school. Keep in mind that whatever you share online will be there for others to see FOREVER! As a middle school student, you will be expected to act responsibly when connecting with other people online.

FINAL THOUGHTS

In **You're Moving on to 6th Grade:** *Easing Your Transition into Middle School,* you have learned about new situations. While this book may not have discussed all issues, some really important ones have been addressed. With all of the seriousness that will come with your life changes, plan to have times that are fun and relaxing, too. Along the way, expect to grow from the new things that you will learn about yourself and others. Cherish the experiences that you will have and the friendships that you will develop. You may find that next year will pass by quicker than you expect. Therefore, take the time to enjoy each day. Hopefully, your 6th grade year will bring many happy memories as you grow into a well-prepared middle school student.

As you move on to 6th grade, use this prayer to continue to *guide* you along the way.

A Serenity Prayer for Students

God, grant me the **SERENITY** to accept and respect myself in spite of what others may think, say, or do, the **COURAGE** to face new situations with a caring heart and a positive attitude, and the **WISDOM** to seek help from trustworthy people who *always* have my best interest and safety in mind. *Amen.*

~Cynthia Bohannon-Brown~

Serenity is a feeling of inner peace and calmness. It eases the nervous feelings in your body and your mind.
Courage is the ability to do something difficult even though you may be afraid.
Wisdom is the ability to consistently make good choices that have positive results. It's usually based on experiences and knowledge.

When you need *motivation and inspiration*, read these words out loud.

AFFIRMATIONS OF HOPE

I have a purpose in this world that goes beyond my everyday life in middle school. The *specialness* in me doesn't live in any other person. Only I own my God-given gifts. With these truths, I promise to be tougher than any unkind words, stronger than a hurt heart, and more positive than all of the negative things that I experience. I know that nothing or no one will stop me from reaching my purpose. I will push through each day. I will keep going when it's hard because eventually I will find my way. I will reach the goals in this world that are uniquely mine. I will stay focused. I will stay hope-filled and I will keep moving FORWARD!

~Cynthia Bohannon-Brown~

APPENDIX – Chart A

You will find additional responsibilities for school personnel listed in these charts.

Responsibilities of Instructional Faculty Chart

Job Title	Examples of Responsibility
Middle School Principal (Administrator)	<ul><li>responsible for the daily operation of the middle school</li><li>serves as a leader and role model for faculty, staff, parents and students</li><li>guides all faculty and staff in performing their jobs correctly and professionally</li><li>acts as the lead teacher</li><li>ensures the safety of everyone in the building</li><li>represents you and your school in the community</li><li>cares for the emotional and physical well-being of all students in the school</li></ul>
Assistant Principal (Administrator)	<ul><li>serves as a co-leader and acts as a role model for faculty, staff and students</li><li>is responsible for the school environment in the Principal's absence</li><li>accepts duties assigned by the Principal</li><li>represents the school in activities, when the Principal is unavailable</li><li>works with discipline and behavior issues</li><li>serves as the contact for the transportation department (buses, etc.)</li><li>cares for the emotional and physical well-being of all students in the school</li></ul>
Teachers (faculty) *This category includes general education, as well as P.E., Art, Music/Band, Technology, ESOL (English to Speakers of Other Languages), Special Education and other teachers.	<ul><li>serve as leaders and role models for other faculty, staff, parents and students.</li><li>guide students through approved course content or information</li><li>use homework, quizzes, and tests to guide students' learning</li><li>listen to concerns from students and helps to find solutions</li><li>plan extra activities and field trips to support content information</li><li>care for the emotional and physical well-being of all students in the class/school</li></ul>

Media Specialist (Faculty)	<ul><li>manages the use of most technology resources</li><li>purchases and organizes all printed library resources</li><li>trains faculty, staff, parents, and students on the proper use of printed materials and technology tools</li><li>compiles and manages technology resources, along with the school's website</li><li>organizes and manages book fairs</li><li>organizes other special events, as needed</li><li>finds support material for teachers</li><li>cares for the emotional and physical well-being of all students in the class/school</li></ul>

CHART A

APPENDIX – Chart B

Responsibilities of Support Staff Chart

Job Title	Examples of Responsibility
Counselor (Staff)	<ul><li>cares for the emotional and physical well-being of all students in the school</li><li>helps students with problems dealing with other people and their personal feelings</li><li>listens to any concerns about stressful situations at home or at school</li><li>keeps conversations between students private and confidential (not allowed to share it with other, unless your safety is involved)</li><li>teaches classes on many different topics dealing with life/school issues and your mental and emotional well-being</li><li>organizes Career Day activities and support other schoolwide events, as needed</li></ul>
Social Worker (Staff)	<ul><li>works with teachers, parents and students to solve issues at home that affect your ability to learn at school ~examples: absences, tardiness, lack of appropriate clothing, abuse/neglect, etc.</li><li>identifies community resources based on the needs of students and their families</li><li>cares for the emotional and physical well-being of all students in the school</li></ul>

Front Office Staff	<ul><li>is key to good communication between the school's administrators, teachers, students, parents, and the community</li><li>sends letters and notes to parents about school events</li><li>answers school-related questions for parent, students and teachers</li><li>connects parents and teachers, during school hours</li><li>is key to the overall operation and safety of the school environment</li><li>connects the school with the district's transportation department during morning and afternoon transportation of students to and from school, as well as during field trips and other off-campus events</li><li>cares for the emotional and physical well-being of all students in the school</li></ul>
Nurse (Staff)	<ul><li>helps students and adults who are ill (sick) or injured (hurt)</li><li>help with emergency medical situations</li><li>informs students about ways to stay healthy</li><li>explains the different ways students' bodies may grow and develop, during the middle school years</li><li>is available for one-on-one discussions about your physical well-being (related to your body)</li><li>cares for the emotional and physical well-being of all students in the school</li></ul>

CHART B

APPENDIX – Chart C

Responsibilities of Support Staff Chart

Job Title	Examples of Responsibility
SRO Staff (School Resource Officers)	• works with administrators, staff, teachers, parents, and students to maintain a safe school environment • leads the school environment during emergency situations • monitors activities during transitions or changes between classes • talks with students about concerns about safe/unsafe behavior or situations • serves as a leader and role model for administrators, teachers, staff, parents, and students • cares for the emotional and physical well-being of all students in the school
Custodians (Staff)	• ensure the safety of the school environment (all areas of the building and the school grounds) • keep all areas clean and in good working order • repair items that are broken • keep school grounds neat and inviting to the community • assist the administrators and SRO staff during drills and emergency situations • care for the emotional and physical well-being of all students in the school
Cafeteria Staff	• serves balanced meals (breakfast and lunch) in a timely manner • keeps the food areas clean and safe • stores all food and non-food items properly • ensures that all children have access to meals on a daily basis • cares for the emotional and physical well-being of all students in the school
Bookkeeper (Staff)	• maintains proper accounting records (information about money/funds) for the school • is responsible for collecting all money for field trips • is responsible for submitting information to payroll for faculty and staff • cares for the emotional and physical well-being of all students in the school

Bus Drivers (Staff)	<ul><li>drive school buses (safely)</li><li>monitor activities on school buses</li><li>ensure that students take the correct buses home each day</li><li>ensure that students are treated with respect</li><li>maintain safe school bus environments</li><li>train students on correct ways to handle emergency situations</li><li>care for the emotional and physical well-being of all students on buses</li></ul>

CHART C

ACKNOWLEDGEMENTS

My heart is filled with thanksgiving and gratitude to the following:

~ To my God, my Creator & my Co-Author, who loves me as my Father, as Jesus, and as the Holy Spirit within me,

~ To my Mom, Dot - editor extraordinaire, for her unconditional love and support,

~ To my Grandparents, the late Thomas Edward Hines Sr. and the late Louise Hill Hines for providing me with a place to call home and for loving me without reservations or judgment,

~ To my family for acknowledging me as a unique individual,

~ To all students who have shared smiles, hugs and experiences over the years, along with those who gave their honest thoughts & concerns about middle school, and

~ To comedian and businessman, Steve Harvey, for his radio and television presence which encouraged & inspired me to JUMP towards my dream of becoming an author and inspirational presenter.

I give a SPECIAL "Thank you!" to the following family and friends for their assistance with editing and proofreading this book:

~Lesley D. Bohannon – my niece who motivated me to fine-tuned my thoughts for this project,

~Marion A. (Starling) Bohannon - my sister-in-law & dear friend who has listened to my dreams of writing and publishing books for over 30 years,

~ Darrell E. Brewster – a giving teacher and a compassionate father,

~ Glenda Easterling – a fellow writer who has given me support, laughter, and a different perspective on life for so many years,

~ Tiffany M. Elston, an extraordinary teacher and "roommate", for her steadfast belief in my ability to complete this project, as well as for her unwavering love and support for our students,

~ LaShawn (Cook) Smith, loving mother and my oldest friend from North Fulton High School – the BEST High School Atlanta, Georgia ever operated!

~ Irwin James – an exceptional photographer & friend from THE North Fulton High School, and

~ Vickie Weaver ~ an inspirational friend, entrepreneur, and spiritual guide.
ALL OF YOU ARE TRULY APPRECIATED!

ABOUT THE AUTHOR

Photo Courtesy of Irwin James Photography

Cynthia Bohannon-Brown, the self-appointed "Queen of Transitions", has had a life filled with changes. She has lived in four different U.S. States and attended 9 different schools from elementary through college. Cynthia has earned four degrees in the areas of: Culinary Arts, Hotel, Restaurant, Travel Administration, Early Childhood Education, and Educational Leadership.

For more than three decades, Cynthia has built a solid foundation of experiences in many different fields. She has worked for several well-known companies, including: Six Flags over Georgia, Delta Airlines, the Internal Revenue Service (IRS), the University of Georgia, Georgia Institute of Technology (Georgia Tech), and Marriott Hotels to name only a few of them. She became a certified Georgia teacher in 1997 and has taught elementary school in two states and in 5 different school systems. Cynthia has worked with students from Kindergarten through 5th grade, including students in Special Education and ESOL (English to Speakers of Other Languages) programs.

To date, Cynthia's most rewarding career has been as an elementary teacher. In that position, she has empowered students to become independent learners and critical thinkers. She plans to continue helping students make their own smooth transitions in school and in life as an educator, author, and inspirational speaker.

"Life is about conquering fears, positively working through changes, and moving forward with living."
                                                    ~Cynthia Bohannon-Brown~

AUTHOR'S CONTACT INFORMATION:

Cynthia Bohannon-Brown, Ed. M.

Educator, Author,
Educational Empowerment Coach &
Inspirational Presenter

Web Page:
www.cbrownteaches.com

Email:
cbrownteaches@gmail.com

www.ingramcontent.com/pod-product-compliance
Lightning Source LLC
Chambersburg PA
CBHW041425090426

42741CB00002B/34